OXFORD ENGLISH

Grad

STORIES
AESO

RAS AL HAMRA SCHOOL

OXFORD ENGLISH PICTURE READERS
COLOUR EDITION

STORIES FROM AESOP

Retold by GWENDOLINE DUN

Illustrated by FRANK C. PAPE

HONG KONG
OXFORD UNIVERSITY PRESS
KUALA LUMPUR SINGAPORE TOKYO

Oxford University Press

OXFORD LONDON GLASGOW
NEW YORK TORONTO MELBOURNE AUCKLAND
KUALA LUMPUR SINGAPORE HONG KONG TOKYO
DELHI BOMBAY CALCUTTA MADRAS KARACHI
NAIROBI DAR ES SALAAM CAPE TOWN SALISBURY
and associates in
BEIRUT BERLIN IBADAN MEXICO CITY NICOSIA

ISBN 0 19 581124 0

Printed in Hong Kong by Hoi Kwong Printing Co.
Published by Oxford University Press, Warwick House, Quarry Bay, Hong Kong

Contents

Aesop lived in Greece many hundreds of years ago. He was the servant of a rich man. He was clever at making up stories and telling them to his friends. Everybody liked hearing the stories he told. Mothers and fathers told them to their children. Travellers heard the stories in Greece and told them in other countries. Aesop became famous all over the world, and his stories are still told today. Here are some of them.

Papé

THE GREEDY DOG

A greedy dog went into a butcher's shop and stole a big juicy bone. He ran away so fast that the butcher could not catch him. He ran out into the fields with his bone. He was going to eat it all by himself.

The dog came to a stream. There was a narrow bridge across it. The dog walked on to the bridge, and looked into the water. He could see his own shadow in the water. He thought it was another dog with a big bone in his mouth.

The greedy dog thought the bone in the water looked much bigger than the one he had stolen from the butcher.

The greedy dog dropped the bone from his mouth. It fell into the water and was lost. He jumped into the water to snatch the bigger bone from the other dog.

The greedy dog jumped into the water with a big splash. He looked everywhere but he could not see the other dog. His shadow had gone.

The silly dog went home hungry.
He lost his bone and got nothing because
he had been too greedy.

THE TOWN MOUSE AND THE COUNTRY MOUSE

A country mouse lived in a field of barley. He made a nest and hung it upon two stalks of barley. The nest was very small and very light. It was made of grass.
The country mouse ate barley and the roots of other plants.

A mouse from the town came to see the country mouse. The town mouse was very quick and clever. His coat was smooth and shining. His home was in a big house in the town.

The country mouse gave the town mouse dinner in the barley field. He brought out the very best barley and roots for the meal. But the town mouse did not enjoy his dinner.

'My poor friend,' he said, 'in town we have much nicer food than this. You must come to see where I live. I shall give you all sorts of good things to eat.'

The town mouse returned to his home in the town. The country mouse went with him. They went to a big house.

'I live here,' said the town mouse. He pointed to a small hole in the wall. 'That is my front door. Come and see my house.'

The town mouse scampered through the hole in the wall. The country mouse followed. They went into a big room. A thick carpet was on the floor. There were beautiful chairs and small tables.

'This is the drawing room,' said the town mouse. 'Sometimes I sleep in the cupboard. We shall eat in the dining room.'

They scampered into another room. There was a long table in it. 'Jump up,' said the town mouse. 'You can eat anything you like.' The town mouse climbed up the table leg, and on to the table. The country mouse followed.

On the table the country mouse saw plates of bread and butter, jam and honey, and cheese. There was a cake full of currants and raisins. Another cake had icing on it, and there were different kinds of biscuits. A jug of water stood in the middle of the table.

The country mouse took a sip of honey. Then he nibbled a small piece of cake. He had never eaten anything so good.

Suddenly the door opened. The two mice jumped off the table, and hid under it. The country mouse was very frightened. A woman came in. She put another cake on the table. She did not see the mice, and she went away.

After a long time, the town mouse and the country mouse climbed back on to the table. The country mouse began to nibble another piece of cake.

Then they heard a dog barking. The dog ran into the room and began to sniff all round the table.

The mice hid behind a big cake. The woman came back.

'Naughty dog!' she said. 'You must not steal the cakes.' She chased the dog out of the room.

The town mouse began to eat again. 'We must hurry,' he said. 'I am not afraid of the dog, but there is a cat here too.'

But the country mouse was running away. 'No thank you,' he said. 'I am going home. This house is too dangerous for me. My house is small, and my food is plain, but I can live in peace and quiet.'

The country mouse went back to his home in the field of barley. He was happy with all his family around him.

THE FOX AND THE GRAPES

A hungry fox was walking along a road one day. He saw some lovely bunches of grapes hanging over a high wall. He stopped to look at the grapes. They looked very good to eat.

The grapes were very high up. The fox stood on his hind legs and put his front paws on the wall. But the grapes were still too far away. He could not reach them.

The fox jumped up as high as he could.
He wanted to eat the grapes very much,
but he could not reach them.

He jumped higher and higher. Sometimes
his nose touched a grape, but he could
not bite one off.

The fox jumped and jumped until he was very tired.

At last he stopped jumping and walked away with his nose in the air.

'I don't want those grapes,' he said. 'I thought they were ripe, but now I am sure they are very sour.'

THE MAN WHO TRIED TO
PLEASE EVERYBODY

One fine morning a farmer went to town to sell his donkey. His son went with him. The farmer led the donkey, and his son walked beside him. They sang as they walked along.

The farmer and his son passed some girls on the road. The girls began to laugh at them.

'What is wrong with your donkey ?' asked
the girls.
'Nothing,' replied the farmer. 'I am going
to sell him in town for a lot of money.'
'You are silly to walk all the way,' said the
girls. 'Let your little boy ride.'
The farmer wanted to please the girls. He
lifted his son on to the donkey, and
walked on beside them.

Farther along the road, the farmer and his son met an old man. The old man shook his stick at the boy. 'What a selfish boy you are,' he cried, 'riding the donkey while your poor father walks.'

To please the old man, the farmer lifted down his son and got on to the donkey himself.

As they went on their way, the farmer and
his son met some women and children.
One of the women pointed to the farmer.
'Look at that lazy man!' she said. 'He
rides the donkey and makes his poor little
boy walk!'
To please the woman, the farmer helped
his son to get up behind him.

The farmer and his son rode along together
on the donkey. They passed some men.
'Is that your donkey?' the men asked.
'You will kill him if you make him carry
a heavy man and a boy. Why don't you
carry the poor donkey?'

The farmer wanted to please the men. He
and his son got off the donkey. They tied
his legs together and slung him on a pole.
The poor donkey struggled and kicked.

The farmer and his son put the ends of
the pole on their shoulders. They walked
into the town carrying the donkey.

The people in the town laughed to see a
man and a boy carrying a struggling
donkey. They ran along beside the farmer
and his son, laughing and shouting.

The poor donkey was frightened. The farmer and his son were tired and hot. They put down the donkey. The beast kicked himself free, and galloped away. He fell into the river and was drowned.

The farmer went home sadly.

'I tried to please everybody,' he said to his son. 'But I have pleased nobody, and I have lost my donkey.'

Papé

THE LION AND THE MOUSE

A lion fell asleep in his den one afternoon.
He had eaten a big dinner. A cheeky
little mouse ran into the lion's den.
He jumped on to the lion's nose, and ran
up to the top of his head.

The lion woke up. He was very angry. He roared loudly, and caught the mouse in his paw.

'How dare you wake me up !' the lion roared. 'I shall kill you for that.'

The mouse was terrified. 'Please, please let me go,' he cried. 'I did not mean to wake you up. Do not kill me. Perhaps one day I shall be able to help you.'

'What?' said the lion. 'How could a tiny animal like you help the King of all the Beasts?'

The lion thought this was very funny. He laughed and let the mouse go free.

'All right, mouse,' he said. 'Run away.'

The mouse slipped out of the lion's paw and scampered away.

One day some hunters spread a net in the forest to catch wild animals. The lion was caught in the net. He struggled hard to get free. He rolled on the ground, but the net wound round and round him. Soon he could not move.

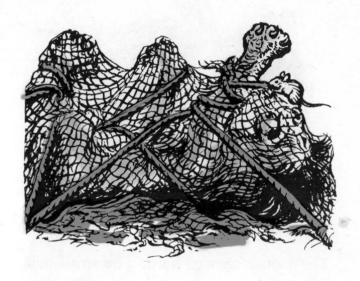

The mouse heard the lion roaring and growling. He ran to see what had happened. 'Lie still,' he said to the lion. 'I shall set you free.'

The mouse had sharp little teeth. He worked very hard and began to chew through the net. Soon he had made a small hole.

The mouse chewed hard. The small hole in the net became a big hole. The lion could move one paw. The mouse went on chewing. Soon the lion could move another paw. Then he was able to stand up. The mouse had set him free!

'There,' said the mouse. 'You laughed at me when I promised to help you. Now you see that a little mouse can help a great lion.'

THE LION AND THE MOUSE

Papé

THE THIRSTY CROW

One hot day, a crow was very thirsty and wanted a drink of water. It was a long way to the river and she was too tired to fly there for a drink. She could not see a pool of water anywhere. She flew round and round. At last she saw a big jug outside a house.

The crow flew down to the jug. She looked inside. There was a little water at the bottom of the jug.

The crow put her head into the jug, but she could not reach the water with her beak. She climbed on to the jug. She almost fell into it, but she could not put her beak into the water.

The crow flew into the air, then she flew
down at the jug and tried to break it with
her beak. But the jug was strong. It would
not break.

The crow flew at the jug, flapping her wings. She tried to knock it over, so that the water would run out on to the ground. But the jug was too heavy. It did not fall over. The crow was too tired to fly any more. She thought she was going to die of thirst.

The crow sat down to rest. She thought and she thought. She did not want to die of thirst.

She saw some small stones lying on the ground. She had an idea. She picked up a stone in her beak and dropped it into the jug. Then another, and another. The water rose higher every time a stone fell into the jug.

Soon the jug was nearly full of stones. The water came to the top. The clever crow put her beak into it at last, and had a drink. Where there's a will, there's a way.

THE HARE AND THE TORTOISE

One day a tortoise went for a walk. As he plodded slowly along, he met a hare. The hare was going for a walk too. The hare had long legs. He did not walk. He ran, and jumped, and played about. He stopped to look at the tortoise, and he began to laugh.

'You are a very funny shape!' said the hare to the tortoise. He laughed and laughed. 'Your legs are very short. Is that why you walk so slowly? Look at my legs. They are very long. I can run very fast.'
'I like to walk slowly,' said the tortoise, 'but perhaps I can get to the top of the hill as soon as you can'.

'What?' said the hare. 'Do you want to run a race with me?' He laughed so much that he fell on the ground. He lay on the grass, laughing and kicking his legs in the air.

'Don't laugh too soon,' said the tortoise.
'Here is a fox. I shall ask him to start the
race. We shall see who finishes first.'
'Ha, ha!' laughed the hare. 'This will be
fun.'
The fox started the race.
'One, two, three — Go!' he shouted.

When the fox shouted 'Go !' the hare gave
a big jump and bounded away as fast as
he could. The tortoise started walking
slowly. Soon he was a long way behind
the hare.

Half way up the hill, the hare stopped and looked back. The tortoise was creeping slowly along in the distance.

The hare laughed. He thought he was very clever. He nibbled some grass, and he played about.

'That tortoise will take a long time to get to the top of the hill,' he said to himself. 'I'll have a rest.'

The hare lay down on the grass and fell sound asleep.

The tortoise plodded slowly on and on. He did not hurry, but he never stopped walking.

After a long time, he passed the hare lying asleep. The tortoise smiled, and went on walking.

After a while, the hare woke up. He looked
behind him for the tortoise. The tortoise
was not there. The hare looked all round
about. At last he saw the tortoise, nearly at
the top of the hill. The hare jumped up,
and bounded away as fast as he could.

The fox stood at the top of the hill. The tortoise got there first. In the distance he saw the hare bounding along.

The hare came hurrying up, out of breath. The tortoise looked at him and smiled. 'You have fine long legs,' he said, 'but they did not get you here so fast as my short legs. Slow and steady wins the race !'

Papé

THE BOY WHO CRIED 'WOLF!'

Some people who lived in a village had a fine flock of sheep. These villagers were frightened of a wolf who lived in the forest. The wolf was always trying to steal the sheep and eat them. The men of the village drove the wolf away many times.

The villagers gave money to a boy.

'Drive the sheep to the grass fields outside the village,' they said to the boy. 'Watch them carefully all day, and look out for the wolf. If you see the wolf, shout to us for help.'

They did not know that this boy liked to play tricks.

Very soon the boy ran to the village.
'Help !' he called. 'Wolf ! Wolf !'
Some men were working on a farm. They
heard the boy shouting.
'We are coming !' they cried.
They picked up pitchforks and rakes. They
ran to save the boy and the sheep from the
wolf.

66

The men ran as fast as they could. When they came to the shepherd boy, they could not see the wolf. The sheep were quietly eating grass.

The boy laughed and laughed.

'That was a good joke,' he said. 'There are no wolves here. The sheep are quite safe. You have run for nothing.'

The men were very angry. But the boy thought he had been very clever.

The next day, the boy drove the sheep to
the other side of the village. He saw some
women getting water at a well.

'Help !' he shouted. 'I see a wolf !'

The women heard the boy shout.

'We must help that poor boy,' they said.

Some of the women picked up sticks and
stones.

Others took off their scarves and shawls,
and waved them in the air. They ran to
help the boy.

The boy saw the women coming. He laughed and pointed.

'How silly you look!' he cried. 'There is no wolf here. I was playing a trick on you.'

'You naughty boy!' cried the women. 'Wait till we catch you!' They began to run after the boy. But the boy ran away from the angry women. They could not catch him.

The boy was very pleased with himself.
He thought his trick was very funny.
But one day a wolf did attack his sheep.
The boy could not drive it away.
'Help!' he cried. 'Help! Wolf! Wolf! A
wolf is attacking the sheep!'

The boy ran to the village, shouting 'Help! Help!'.

But nobody would listen to him.

'He is playing a trick on us again,' they all said.

The wolf killed many of the sheep. The boy had played his silly trick too often. The men caught him and beat him till he cried.

THE NORTH WIND
AND THE SUN

One day, the North Wind met the Sun. They began to quarrel.

The North Wind is a cold wind. It howls loudly and is very strong. It brings rain and snow.

'I am stronger than you,' the North Wind said to the Sun. 'I can blow down big trees. I can blow the roofs off houses. I can make big waves on the sea.'

'No, I am stronger than you,' said the Sun quietly. 'I can melt ice and snow. I can draw up water from the sea to make clouds. I make the trees and flowers grow.'

A man came walking along, wearing a big cloak.

'Look at that man,' cried the North Wind. 'I can blow off his cloak. You can't do that.'

The North Wind blew hard at the man. The man's cloak blew open.

The North Wind blew harder. The man felt cold. He did up his cloak and turned up the hood. The North Wind howled and blew harder still. The man was nearly blown off the road. But he put his head down. He put his hands in the pockets of his cloak, and he kept on walking. The wind could not blow off his cloak.

The Sun smiled.

'Now watch me!' it said. 'I'll show you a better way to take off the man's cloak.'

The Sun came out from behind a cloud. It shone down on the man. The man felt warm, and turned down the hood of his cloak.

'That is nothing,' said the North Wind. 'The man is still wearing his cloak.'

'Wait,' said the Sun. 'I have not finished.' It shone more strongly upon the man. The man began to feel hot. He looked up at the sky.

'The sun is shining,' he said, 'and the wind has gone. I will take off my cloak.'

He undid his cloak and took it off.

The man put his cloak over his arm and walked away. The Sun laughed.

'You are very strong,' he said to the North Wind, 'but I took off the man's cloak.'

The North Wind howled angrily, and rushed away to the hills.

Persuasion is better than force.